BEST 15 COMPILED ESSAYS

Shobhit Trivedi

BLUEROSE PUBLISHERS
U.K.

Copyright © Shobhit Trivedi 2025

All rights reserved by author. No part of this publication may be reproduced, stored in a retrieval system or transmitted in any form or by any means, electronic, mechanical, photocopying, recording or otherwise, without the prior permission of the author. Although every precaution has been taken to verify the accuracy of the information contained herein, the publisher and the author assumes no responsibility for any errors or omissions. No liability is assumed for damages that may result from the use of information contained within.

BlueRose Publishers takes no responsibility for any damages, losses, or liabilities that may arise from the use or misuse of the information, products, or services provided in this publication.

For permissions requests or inquiries regarding this publication, please contact:

BLUEROSE PUBLISHERS
www.BlueRoseONE.com
info@bluerosepublishers.com
+4407342408967

ISBN: 978-93-7018-505-0

Cover design: Daksh
Typesetting: Tanya Raj Upadhyay

First Edition: June 2025

Preface: -

It gives me great pleasure to present this compiled edition of essays in the form of a book. What began as a personal effort to express and explore ideas has gradually developed into a thoughtfully curated collection that I am proud to share with readers. Each essay reflects both intellectual inquiry and sincere engagement with subjects that I hope will resonate with a wide audience.

To make the content more accessible, especially for students, I have included key points alongside the essays. These are intended to help readers quickly understand the core message and deeper insights within each piece. The book has gone through several rounds of careful revision to ensure clarity, coherence, and overall excellence.

As a student and a first-time author, this journey has been both challenging and rewarding. I am deeply grateful to the dedicated publishing team whose support made this book possible. Their guidance and encouragement were invaluable at every step of the process.

I also extend my heartfelt thanks to my family, especially my grandmother ("Daadi"), whose constant love and support have been my greatest strength throughout this endeavour.

With sincere gratitude, I present this book to its readers, and I hope it offers both knowledge and inspiration.

About the Author: -

The author of this book, Shobhit Trivedi, is a passionate and aspiring individual currently residing in Kanpur, Uttar Pradesh. As a student, he has taken a significant step into the educational landscape by publishing his very first book. This debut work marks the beginning of his journey in the academic and literary domain. Shobhit's motivation behind writing and publishing this book stems from a sincere commitment to the welfare of students. His goal is to contribute meaningfully to the educational development of learners by offering valuable insights through his writing. With a strong belief in the power of education, he aims to inspire and support fellow students in their academic pursuits.

Contact Details of the Author:

Readers are welcome to reach out to the author for any queries, feedback or discussions by emailing him at: shobhittrivedi123@outlook.com.

Table of Contents

"Digital Libraries are better than Traditional Libraries" 1

"Electric Vehicles are better than Fuel-Operated Vehicles" 11

"Railways are the best means of transportation in India" 22

"School Examinations are very beneficial for students" 33

"A.I. is a blessing for India" 42

"Online classes are better than offline classes" 52

"Rainwater harvesting is the need of the hour" 63

"Rural areas and Population Explosion" 69

"Impact of social media on teenagers" 75

"UPI shall be made as the only mode of Payment" .. 80

"C.C.T.V. cameras must be installed in every classroom" 86

"Parents should not be strict to their children" 92

"Role and benefits of Television in the society" 96

"Increasing Global Warming is a Warning" 102

"Privatization and its Impact" 107

"DIGITAL LIBRARIES ARE BETTER THAN TRADITIONAL LIBRARIES"

For the motion

A place where a number of books are kept for different topics and subjects is called Library. Libraries have a large collection of several books which can be issued for a limited time period and then returned back to them. Libraries are buildings which play a major role in spreading knowledge to masses. But as according to Newton's third law which states that "every action has an equal and opposite reaction", there is also a reaction in response to the action of these libraries. The reaction metaphorically refers to the loss caused to our environment by these libraries. In this reference, digital libraries are the libraries which neither have any building nor do they have any physical book. They are based on the books that are uploaded to their database through the internet.

The introduction of the concept of digital libraries has also proved itself to be a boon for the nature and its constituents. Libraries contain a large number of books, and each book contains a large number of pages, these pages are manufactured from trees. And as we all know, trees are the basic unit which helps almost all the living things in their survival. The digital libraries do not cause much harm to the surroundings as they run on the principle of uploading entire book on platforms through which the readers can access the books. As there are no physical pages required, activities like deforestation can be reduced and the forest cover throughout the globe can be increased. This will result in helping the global population in reducing the air pollution as well as global warming.

Libraries are buildings which contain books. These buildings have limited quantity of seats, books and space for the readers whereas the digital libraries offer a wide range of books as well as they do not require any building or any other space. So, readers can easily read books with the help of their own mobile phones or other supported digital devices.

Physical libraries use electricity, water and other resources. And the charges for using these resources are included in the fees of the libraries. Hence these physical libraries fail to prove themselves more economically fit than digital libraries.

Physical libraries are immovable. Readers are required to move to the libraries in order to read books. But digital libraries do not require such activities. They can be accessed even from the home of each and every reader. Hence, these libraries prevent the pollution caused by burning of fossil fuels to operate the vehicles or to provide electricity for operation of the electric vehicles for going to physical libraries. Even while travelling, digital libraries can easily be accessed. This saves the time wasted while travelling and increases the interest of the readers towards books.

Further, the time for accessing the traditional libraries is often regulated, whereas these digital libraries are open to their readers all the time.

Hence with this, I would like to end my composition emphasizing the benefits of using digital libraries over physical libraries.

Against the motion

The modern approach of people towards books is decreasing day-by-day. The impact of which can easily be seen on the youth. The busy lifestyle of today's era does not allow individuals to spend their time in reading books. Although books are our best friends who guide us throughout our life. In order to allow readers to read and continue this process of reading, the concept of digital libraries was introduced. This concept allows the readers to read books any time they wish. But, instead of helping, this method has also caused harm to the readers.

The use of mobile phones, laptops, desktop P.C.s or tablets to read books helps the readers in accessing the book from anywhere and anytime they wish. But it causes harm to the eyesight and mental well-being of the readers also. Scientific studies have found that, the blue light emitted from the screens of such devices produces stress in eyes and continuous exposure to these lights delays the secretion of melatonin hormone from the pineal gland of our brain. This hormone is very crucial for the regulation of the sleep cycle. Hence when the sleep cycle is disturbed, it results in decrease in the mental ability of a person to do any work.

The modern devices, which are used for accessing digital libraries, are also source to many other types of applications other than the digital libraries. While reading books through these devices, the concentration of the readers easily gets disturbed due to notifications or calls from different sources. This reduces the retentive capacity of the brain of readers.

These digital libraries allow the readers to read books after taking subscriptions, but they fail to check that whether the number of readers reading the book from the same device is restricted to only one reader or not. This results in decrease in overall revenue and the share of the writer of respective book.

For accessing these digital libraries, mobile, laptop, computer or tablets along-with internet are required. But still in our nation, there are many places where internet is not available constantly. So, the students of those areas cannot access digital libraries.

Further, a physical library requires a number of workers such as librarian, sweeper and so on. If we shift on the concept of digital libraries, these workers will be deprived of their wages and they will lose their jobs. This will increase the unemployment rate of the country too.

So, with this I would like to end my essay making this very point clear that the new concept of library can never defeat the traditional method.

Important points of the composition for the motion: -

1. Digital libraries offer a vast range of books for the readers to read as per their wish.
2. Digital libraries do not require electricity, furniture, water and other resources for the readers. Hence the overall fee charged for these resources is reduced. This makes digital libraries more economically fit than physical libraries.
3. Physical libraries are immovable. Hence, readers are required to move to the libraries in order to study books.
4. Digital libraries prevent the pollution caused by burning of fossil fuels to operate the vehicles, or to provide electricity for operation of the vehicles for going to physical libraries.
5. The time for accessing the traditional libraries is often regulated whereas digital libraries are open to their readers all the time.
6. Physical libraries can accommodate a given number of readers at a time. Whereas digital libraries can allow thousands of readers to read books all the time.
7. Traditional libraries contain books which are made up of a large number of pages. These pages are made from the wood pulp of the trees whereas digital libraries do not require pages.

8. The reduction in cutting-off of the trees will favour our atmosphere.
9. Digital libraries can be accessed even while travelling.
10. The physical libraries cause discomfort to the readers as they are restricted to the limited number of books present in the library.

Important points of the composition against the motion: –

1. Digital libraries always require use of electronic gadgets like mobile, laptop, desktop or tablet.
2. The blue light emitted from the screens of these electronic gadgets poses harm to the eyesight of the readers.
3. Continuous exposure to these lights delays the secretion of melatonin hormone from the pineal gland of our brain.
4. Melatonin hormone is very crucial for the regulation of the sleep cycle.
5. While reading books through these devices, the concentration of the readers is disturbed due to notifications or calls from difference sources.
6. This disturbance reduces the retentive capacity of the brain of readers.
7. These digital libraries allow the readers to read books after taking subscriptions, but they cannot check whether the number of readers reading the book from the same device is restricted to only one reader or not.
8. In our nation there are many places where internet is not available constantly.
9. If we shift on the concept of digital libraries, workers of physical libraries will be deprived of their wages and they will lose their jobs.

10. Removal of workers from libraries to give way to digital libraries to be setup will increase the unemployment rate of the country too.

"ELECTRIC VEHICLES ARE BETTER THAN FUEL-OPERATED VEHICLES"

For the motion

The invention of vehicles has proved itself to be a blessing for the human beings. It is because of vehicles only that the people are able to travel long distances in a very less time. Till now, Indian vehicular industry is being dominated by fuel-operated vehicles which run either on petrol or on diesel. But in recent few years, the craze for electrically-operated vehicles is also rising among the Indian population.

Nowadays, the electrically operated vehicles are being preferred more over the petrol or diesel operated vehicles as the charges of these fuels are increasing day by day. This is because the fuels used in fuel-operated vehicles are derived from the fossils which are obtained from the inner surface of the Earth. We have to understand, that these fuels are present in a limited quantity inside the surface of the Earth. As the rate of consumption of these fuels is increasing, the fuels are depleting. Hence to take out more fuel from the inner deep surface of the Earth, more complicated machineries are used which lead to increase in the cost of these fuels. This makes these fuels more expensive in comparison to electricity.

Further, battery-operated vehicles do not have parts such as engine and fuel injectors. This helps in decreasing the maintenance cost of these vehicles as they have only basic motors and a battery which provides energy to these motors. That is why these electric vehicles do not cause pollution while running hence they also help us by reducing the harm caused to our environment. Whereas, the petrol or diesel operated vehicles have internal combustion engines with several other machineries installed in them which release a lot of carbon dioxide as by-product. This carbon dioxide is very harmful for our planet as it is a greenhouse gas and increase in its quantity leads to rise in global temperature of Earth's surface. Also, these engines are more prone to wear and tear because a large amount of heat energy is generated during combustion of fuels in these engines.

The running cost of electric vehicles is less than that of fuel-operated vehicles. This is because of the presence of less machine parts in these vehicles. Hence, a less amount of energy is required to overcome the forces of friction. This increases the efficiency of these vehicles. And the increased efficiency results in increasing the power as well as the average mileage of these vehicles.

Also, because of less machinery used, these vehicles create very less noise while moving as compared to the fuel-operated vehicles. These vehicles disturb neither the mental peace of people moving on the road nor the peaceful elements of the nature.

With this I would like to end my composition indicating the fact that the electric vehicles are better than fuel-operated vehicles for both nature and human beings. So, we should now take a step ahead to promote the use of electric vehicles in place of fuel-operated vehicles for the sake of the future of Earth and its atmosphere.

Against the motion

Ever since the 21st century, the demand for vehicles in India is increasing drastically. This is just because in our nation vehicles are considered as a symbol of prosperity. That is why whenever a new vehicle is launched, people panic to buy that as if there is a race. Same is happening with the battery-operated vehicles in our nation. People are buying these vehicles without understanding that whether these vehicles are worth buying according to current situations or not.

Battery-operated vehicle is a new class of vehicles which have been introduced in recent few years for promoting use of these vehicles and demoting the use of fuel-operated vehicles. These vehicles are being considered better than the fuel-operated vehicles. But according to the current situations this consideration is false.

The reason for calling this consideration false is that, the electrically operated vehicles run on batteries which provide them energy. And after a fixed time period these batteries become useless and their replacement becomes necessary. The cost of replacement of these batteries is almost equal to the average cost of the fuel exhausted while using a fuel-operated vehicle in cities.

Further, the batteries after serving their purposes when are of no use, need to be either recycled with care or disposed-off properly. If these batteries are not disposed-off properly the chemicals or the toxins present in these batteries pose a serious threat to the environment and the soil conditions. As the presence of lithium or lead in the battery ruins the soil making it unsuitable for its natural use.

The batteries of these vehicles need to be recharged before using them. And these batteries also take a lot of time while charging. Hence in case of an emergency, if the vehicle is not charged, it will waste a lot of time in charging the vehicle before going anywhere.

In case, if the battery of these vehicles gets discharged while travelling. It is not easy to locate the charging stations on the highways because these vehicles are not very common or in case if charging stations are found, a lot of time is wasted in getting the vehicle charged. Whereas in comparison to charging stations, fuelling stations can be easily found on the highways and also the time taken in fuelling up a vehicle is also not very much.

Further, in case electric vehicle gets broken down on a highway. It becomes a very tedious task to find out mechanic for electric vehicles and the companies of the vehicles also charge a considerable sum of money for reaching to the location of the vehicle. And as the fuel-operated vehicles are very common, the mechanics for fuel-operated vehicles can easily be found.

So, keeping all the points in view, I would like to end my composition stating that according to the current situations, fuel-operated vehicles are better than battery operated ones until the resources for battery operated vehicles are fully developed.

Important points of the composition for the motion: -

1. Invention of vehicles has proved itself to be a blessing for the human beings.
2. Because of vehicles, it is easier for people to travel long distances in a very less time.
3. As the rate of consumption of these fuels is increasing, the fuels are depleting. Hence to take out more fuel from the inner deep surface of the Earth, more complicated machineries are used which lead to increase in the cost of these fuels.
4. The electrically operated vehicles consist up of less machinery parts and hence less amount of energy is wasted in overcoming the forces of friction in the moving parts.
5. Maintenance cost of electrically-operated vehicles is very less.
6. Petrol or diesel operated vehicles have internal combustion engines. And as a by-product of combustion these engines release a large amount of carbon-dioxide.
7. The carbon-dioxide released as a by-product of combustion in internal combustion engines of fuel-operated vehicles is a source of global warming.
8. Electrically-operated vehicles produce a very less sound as compared to that of fuel-operated vehicles.

9. Electrically-operated vehicles are more environmentally friendly as compared to the fuel-operated vehicles.
10. The average mileage of electric vehicles is more than fuel-operated vehicles.

Important points of the composition against the motion: -

1. People are buying Electric vehicles without understanding that whether these vehicles are worth buying according to current situations or not.
2. The electrically operated vehicles run on batteries which provide them energy and after a fixed time period these batteries become useless.
3. The cost of replacement of these batteries is almost equal to the average cost of fuel exhausted while using a fuel-operated vehicle in cities.
4. After serving their purposes, when batteries are of no use, they need to be either recycled or disposed-off properly.
5. If the batteries of electrically operated vehicles are not disposed-off properly. They pose risk to the environment.
6. It takes a lot of time in recharging the electric vehicles.
7. In case if the batteries of these electric vehicles get drained while moving on a highway, it is very hard to locate charging stations. As these vehicles are not very common, the availability of charging stations is very less.
8. It is very hard to find mechanics of electric vehicles.
9. It wastes a lot of time in charging electric vehicles as compared to the time wasted in refuelling fuel-operated vehicles.

10. Vehicles are considered as a symbol of prosperity in India. Hence people are buying electric vehicles to show their prosperity without understanding that which class of vehicle would suit them the best.

"RAILWAYS ARE THE BEST MEANS OF TRANSPORTATION IN INDIA"

For the motion

Railways have a very long past in India. It was first introduced in our nation by the British government. Since the very beginning, Railways are being liked the most by the citizens of India. The major objects of the railways which contribute in making it a means of transport are Trains, Railway Stations, and the Rails on which these trains run.

The main reason for the railways being liked the most is the economical fitness of the railways with the budget of the Indian citizens. There are multiple categories in the Railway System of India such as general, sleeper, A.C. tier I, A.C. tier II and A.C. tier III. All these categories are offered in a same train and the charges for different categories are also different. This makes it possible for the citizens to choose the category which fits the best as per their income and budget.

Further, the railways offer a large amount of space for sleeping or sitting. This makes the journey more comfortable. Specially for the senior citizens of our nation, the railways are the best means of transportation because of the availability of a large amount of space and legroom. And for the children under specific age, there is no amount charged by the railways. Also, the railways offer restrooms to the citizens so that the journey becomes more comfortable. The railways also provide the citizens with a protection force for their safety. This force is named as Railway Protection Force.

Railways is the most liked means of transport by the citizens of our nation. That is why, most of the population chooses to use railway transport over any other means of transport. This results in increase in the number of tickets booked. Hence the net revenue earned by the railways shows a significant contribution in the total revenue collected by the nation.

Unlike older ones, the modern railway engines run on the electric power. This feature of modern railways helps the natural world in many ways as when these railway engines run on the electrical energy, the fossil fuels present under the surface of the Earth are not used for running these engines. This reduces the cost of refining of petroleum to meet the needs of the people. Also, since these engines do not burn fossil fuels, a large difference in the air pollution caused by the new engines and older engines can be easily observed as new engines which run on electricity produce a negligible amount of pollution.

Further, since railways are more economical means of transport than individual vehicles, when people travel through trains instead of their individual vehicles the net pollution produced in the former case is much less than the latter one.

Trains travel throughout the nation connecting several villages with cities and towns. And they are also not convinced by the climatic or weather conditions. Hence, during droughts or famine kind of situations, the effect of these disasters is reduced to a greater extent because of the railways. Railways also help the less developed regions to use the resources of more developed regions and by this act, the margin of backwardness for the less developed regions is reduced. Railways can also carry postages and a large amount of heavy and bulky goods.

Hence in favour of the topic, with the support of all the points listed about I would like to say that railways are unbeatable mode of transportation in fields of comfort, safety and budget in India till date.

Against the motion

Whenever we ask people to choose a mode of transport for travelling from one place to another. Their first preference always favours the Railways. But in recent few years, it is observed that the railways are not being treated as first preference by most of the masses who can afford means of transport other than railways.

There are several reasons for this, one of the most popular reasons for the railways being not preferred as the best means of transport is the longer time taking journeys of it. Since trains stop multiple times, The time taken in reaching a destination by a train is much more than the time taken by airways. That is why people are preferring air transport over railways. And since railways cannot cross seas and oceans, the transportation of large bulky goods is preferred to be carried out by waterways.

Further, the number of people travelling in a train is always more than the number of berths present in the train as the railways continue to issue tickets even if the capacity of the train is full. These tickets are issued under different sections so that if the reserved tickets get cancelled, these extra tickets would get confirmed. This makes trains crowded and unhygienic as all the tickets do not get cancelled and as people have paid for reservation, they have right to travel. This overcrowding of railways causes people to sit at floor near washroom or at the stairs of the train. Thus, even after having a lot of space, these trains are always small for carrying such a large crowd.

Because of a large population travelling through the means of railways. Many people find shelter in the mass of the crowd and they travel without tickets. Because of huge crowd, it becomes difficult for the railway staff to check the tickets of each and every passenger. Thus, this act of them not only makes trains populated but also causes loss to the country which is equal to the revenue generated for each ticket of the passengers travelling by that train.

The railways not only carry a large number of passengers but it also carries heavy goods. But in absence of proper attention towards the goods, the conditions such as pilferage are the most significant problems which make people choose the roadways for the purpose of transporting essential goods from one place to another.

The railways employ a large number of people. So, it becomes almost impossible to track each and everyone. Few people, who falsely claim themselves to be employees of railways, are often caught taking bribes from people. This reduces the reputation of the Indian railways. It is of utmost importance for the railways to mark a full stop on the process of bribery and also to severely punish the fake or actual officers who promote bribery.

Railways require a flat land terrain to be set-up. This type of land terrain is not available in the hilly regions of northern India. And also, the cost of setting up one kilometre of roadways is less than setting up one kilometre of railways. Thus, it makes railways confined to a definite region only.

With this, I would like to end my composition with all the points listed above against the motion.

Important points of the composition for the motion: -

1. Railways have a very long past in India. It was first introduced in India by the British government.
2. Railways are being liked the most by the citizens of India.
3. The main reason for the railways being liked the most is the economical fitness of the railways with the budget of the Indian citizens.
4. Further, the railways offer a large amount of space for sleeping or sitting. This makes the journey more comfortable.
5. For the senior citizens of our nation, the railways are the best means of transportation because of the availability of a large amount of space and legroom.
6. The railways also provide the citizens with a protection force for their safety. This force is named as Railway Protection Force.
7. The net revenue earned by the railways shows a significant contribution in the total revenue collected by the nation.
8. When people travel through trains instead of their individual vehicles the net pollution produced in the former case is much less than the latter one.
9. Trains travel throughout the nation connecting several villages with cities and towns. And they are also not convinced by the climatic or weather conditions.

10. Railways also help the less developed regions to use the resources of more developed regions and by this act the margin of backwardness for the less developed regions is reduced.

Important points of the composition against the motion: -

1. In recent few years, it is observed that the railways are not being treated as first preference by most of the masses who can afford means of transport other than railways.
2. Railways are slower means of transport as compared to airways.
3. As railways cannot cross seas and oceans, the transportation of large bulky goods is preferred to be carried out by waterways.
4. The number of people travelling in a train is always more than the number of berths present in the train as the railways continue to issue tickets even if the capacity of the train is full.
5. Many people find shelter in the mass of the crowd and they travel without tickets.
6. The act of people travelling without tickets not only makes trains populated but also causes loss to the country which is equal to the revenue generated for each ticket of the passengers travelling by that train.
7. In absence of proper attention towards the goods the conditions such as pilferage are the most significant problems which make people to choose the roadways for the purpose of transporting essential goods from one place to another.

8. Few people, who falsely claim themselves to be employees of railways, are often caught taking bribes.
9. Railways require a flat land terrain to be set-up. This type of land terrain is not available in the hilly regions of northern India. Thus, it makes railways confined to a definite region only.
10. The cost of setting up 1 kilometre of roadways is less than setting up 1 kilometre of railways.

"SCHOOL EXAMINATIONS ARE VERY BENEFICIAL FOR STUDENTS"

For the motion

In our nation, education system is based on the concept of examination in which the scholars of different subjects or topics are tested by asking them questions in both written as well as oral/vocal form. The motion of the topic is against the regular custom of conduction of examination in the school as per the policies adopted by the hon'ble and learned people of the nation. This makes me stand against the motion of the topic and thus favour the policies drafted by the hon'ble and the learned group. If the students succeed in writing or explaining the correct answers, they are considered as passed or qualified for the examinations. The upcoming points will help us in understanding how this method of examining the student is the best way.

In current pattern of examinations, the students are required to answer the questions related to a topic. Which suggests that the student has studied the complete topic, that's why, he/she is easily able to write the answer. This also suggests that the student has obtained knowledge in that particular subject. And hence, the purpose of educating the students is fulfilled by this practice of the teachers.

This method of writing answers to a specific number of questions prevents wastage of time as well as other valuable resources such as paper. As less amount of paper is required to answer limited questions in comparison to the amount required for writing the entire topic. It is easy to test students by asking them difficult questions related to a particular topic. Hence logical thinking ability of students is enhanced by this method. Answers for any question related to a topic can only be given when the respective topic is thoroughly prepared. So, if a student is able to write correct answers to asked questions, this means that the topic has been thoroughly prepared by the students. This helps in enhancing the memory of the student.

Further, when teachers ask questions from any field of the topic or the chapter it makes students learn each and every line, this helps in increasing the focus of the students.

Thus, this way of examination helps teachers in finding out the weak or careless students amongst the mob of the intelligent ones, and hence they gradually make weaker ones also one of the members of the intelligent mob. Further, by the way of examination, the students who show very careless attitude towards their studies also study because of the pressure created by the 'fear of failing' in exams. This method of learning as well as preparing for exams lights up the spirits of students to score good marks as well as this method makes the students disciplined by following same routine daily and daily. Hence school examinations help the students a lot for appearing in successive competitive and life examinations. With this, I want to end my essay expressing heartfelt gratitude towards our teachers.

Against the motion

In our nation, education system is based on the concept of examination. This is one of the reasons for the increase in the rate of unemployment. The rate of suicides committed by the students is also increasing very rapidly. This is an alarming situation which reminds all of us to look forward to change our education policy. In the era of older Indian education system, i.e. when the gurukul system used to dominate over all the parts of country, the examinations were based on the fields of expertise of the students and lessons which people learnt there helped them throughout their life. That's the reason why the students of those times were more efficient in their work. But nowadays, schools have shifted from the practical to ideal approach of studies which is merely based on the ideal concepts and most of them have no resemblance and are also not possible in real life as well.

The current conditions of the students are because of the new concept of schools. As it makes the students good learners not good scholars. This thought becomes the reason for the students failing in the competitive examinations. Schools ask questions for which the answers are written in the books. There is no need to understand and apply the concept about which the question is asked. This makes the student suffer in the particular topic not just because of his/her carelessness but because of lack of conceptual knowledge towards the topic.

Further, the results of the examinations conducted by the school depend upon the questions asked by the teacher or the examiner. If a student has scored good marks in the exams, it simply means that the student knows the answers to the asked questions. And here arises a condition that this may happen that the topper student would not be perfect in each and every part of the topic except the part from where the questions were asked. And also, the student who is not able to score good marks may know the entire topic thoroughly except the part from where the questions were asked. But the results for the same students reduce the self-confidence of the less scoring student and this draws a line of bitterness in their friendly relations. Thus, this decrease in self-confidence of the students is what makes the newspapers to write headings in which friends become the source of causing harm to each other.

In order to make students excel in their lives, the education policy shall be reconstructed in such a way that would allow the students to understand the topics rather than just learning them. And also, to allow them to choose their paths as they wish.

With this I want to end my essay with few lines in support of my opinion which sound as "Gaining education is a road to success unless and until it is not forced to do so."

Important points of the composition for the motion: -

1. In our nation, education system is based on the concept of examination.
2. In the current education system, if the students succeed in writing or explaining the correct answers, they are considered as passed or qualified for the examinations.
3. The questions are asked from almost all the parts of the topic.
4. If the student succeeds in writing correct answers to the questions asked, it implements that the child has read and learnt about that topic thoroughly. Otherwise, he/she would not be able to write the correct answers.
5. If students are able to write correct answer to the asked question. The purpose of educating the students is fulfilled by this practice of the teachers.
6. This method promotes nature by reducing paper usage. As less amount of paper is required to answer limited questions in comparison to the amount required for writing the entire topic.
7. Logical thinking ability of students is enhanced by this method.
8. This also helps in enhancing the memory of the students as it makes students learn each and every line of the chapter.

9. This way of examination helps teachers in finding out the weak or careless students amongst the mob of the intelligent ones.
10. By the way of examination, the students who show very careless attitude towards their studies also study because of the pressure created by the 'fear of failing' in exams.

Important points of the composition against the motion: -

1. In our nation, education system is based on the concept of examination. This is one of the reasons for the increase in the rate of unemployment.
2. When the gurukul system used to dominate over all the parts of country, the lessons which people learnt there helped them throughout their life.
3. Schools have shifted from the practical to ideal approach of studies which is merely based on the ideal concepts and most of them have no resemblance and are also not possible in real life as well.
4. Schools ask questions for which the answers are written in the books.
5. The results of the examinations conducted by the school depend upon the questions asked by the teacher or the examiner.
6. If a student has scored good marks in the exams, it simply means that the student knows the answers to the asked questions.
7. If a student is not able to score good marks, this may happen that he/she knows about the topic but could not answer the questions during the examinations.
8. In order to make students excel in their lives, the education policy shall be reconstructed in such a way that would allow the students to understand the topics rather than just learning them.

9. Modern education system makes the student suffer in the particular topic(s) not just because of his/her carelessness but because of lack of conceptual knowledge towards the topic.
10. "Gaining education is a road to success unless and until it is not forced to do so."

"A.I. IS A BLESSING FOR INDIA"

For the motion

Artificial Intelligence, popularly known as 'A.I.', is a kind of technology which gives personified results to the inputs of its users. The craze for artificial intelligence is increasing day-by-day throughout the world. The reason for this is its flexibility with respect to the needs of the operator. It can easily write on difficult topics, arrange spreadsheet data into required form, write lyrics for songs, provide summaries of chapters, create presentations and many more.

The efficiency of artificial intelligence is increasing rapidly because it collects usage data from the users and uses that data to make itself better. And now, it has evolved to such an extent that making complex computer programs or performing other tedious tasks has become just a cup of tea for people with the help of the artificial intelligence.

After the introduction of Artificial Intelligence, the technological industry has seen many changes. These changes have helped all the sectors in reducing their workload as Artificial Intelligence can perform most of the tasks. This makes it more popular among the masses.

Artificial intelligence has helped a lot in field of education and medicine. Because of Artificial Intelligence, students can easily complete their assignments on time. A.I. acts as a virtual teacher for the students and provides summaries of the topics to make them easier for the students to understand. In case of any doubt, artificial intelligence also clears the doubts of the students in no time. Hence, it is nothing less than a true mentor for students. Further in the fields such as medicinal research or surgeries, A.I. can easily predict the expected outcomes before performing actual experiments.

Artificial intelligence gives responses as a human being. Hence, people find it as their friend. They talk to A.I. and share their issues and feelings with it. A.I. also in return gives the most appropriate advice to its users after analysing the type of issue. This quality of it makes Artificial Intelligence a good friend to its users and by this act, it can reduce the mental stress of its users even being a software.

Many companies have handed over few or more sectors of their management to Artificial Intelligence. A.I. looks after many matters and performs the expected tasks in no times. The best example of the use of Artificial Intelligence can be experienced when, during any conversation, we talk or send messages about specific products it shows us advertisements related to those products only. This type of marketing increases the sales of the companies. And we call this type of marketing as personalized advertisements.

In India, it is used in many fields by the law enforcement departments too. As it can predict the entire face of a person by seeing just one third of the face, it can be used by the local police for finding out convicts. A.I. is also used to control a large amount of population that is why artificial intelligence was also involved in the management of the Maha Kumbh Mela which was held recently in January 2025 in India.

Hence, finalizing my composition, I would like to say that in few decades, with the evolution of A.I., it will become one stop solution for all the problems. This is just because of few unbeatable features of it such as, it never gets tired as well as there are no fixed working hours for it to work, so it can work 24x7. It can perform several tasks together with almost no error. Hence the man-power of the companies or organisations will be reduced, this will help in increasing in the profits of the organisations.

Against the motion

Artificial Intelligence is one of the most common words we hear in 21st century. Although by the 20th century, no one had ever thought about it, but the way it has evolved itself made it a common name in each and every school, office and household. In the beginning it was not given very much attention by people. But after few days, when they all saw the fast evolution of 'A.I' in no time, they too started praising it.

For a layman's point of view, Artificial Intelligence is one of the best experiments in the field of technology. But for a practical approach of thinking, it is of urgent importance to know that Artificial Intelligence is harming us in place of benefitting us.

As Artificial Intelligence can easily do multiple jobs together at the same time, it is reducing the number of employees employed by a company. Many companies are preferring Artificial Intelligence over the talented employees. This feature of A.I. is thus making it a source for increase in the rate of unemployment throughout the nation. Also because of the increase in unemployment, the salaries paid to the employees reduces, and hence the amount of income tax given to the nation also decreases. This reduction in tax acts as a barrier in the smooth development of our nation and its resources.

Artificial Intelligence can create a number of computer program in several computer languages in a very negligible amount of time. This results in the reduction of job opportunities for the same computer engineers who invented Artificial Intelligence, as the companies prefer A.I. over them since it can create multiple clones of itself too in no time. Hence the time invested by the computer engineers for studying their courses and then building A.I. is wasted.

Artificial intelligence is capable of creating images, videos and many other elements which is used by the criminals in generating deepfake images and videos of innocent people. This act of them creates a lot of disturbance in the practical and mental life of the victims. Also, the drawings and arts created by the artificial intelligence make many artists jobless.

For getting any service from the Artificial Intelligence, many times people enter their personal data into it. This data is usually stored by the 'A.I.' for carrying out its development according to the inputs and recommendations made by its users. This stored data can be easily stolen by the criminals and hence it can result in some or the other mishappening. It is seen that after the introduction of Artificial Intelligence the rate of cybercrimes has shown a sharp rise. This situation is alarming for us. And we should, by ourselves, regulate the use of Artificial Intelligence.

With this, I would like to end my composition indicating towards the fact that, we should keep in mind that the invention of Artificial intelligence is done by human beings only. So, it can never be as smart and intelligent as its developers, but still if it is given a chance by not handling it with care and precautions, it is not impossible that by the power of self-cloning, it can increase its powers to such an extent that it would start dominating over human subjects.

Important points of the composition for the motion: –

1. Artificial intelligence is popularly known as 'A.I.'.
2. The craze for artificial intelligence is evolving day by day.
3. The artificial intelligence collects data from the users and uses that data to make itself better.
4. Artificial intelligence has proved itself to be a boon for educational industry as it acts as a virtual teacher and can solve the doubts of students related to various subjects or topics.
5. A.I. can predict the results of the researches before performing the experiment actually.
6. Artificial intelligence gives human like responses. Hence, people find it relaxing to share their personal problems without the fear of being getting leaked. This property helps the A.I. in reducing the stress of its users.
7. Artificial intelligence has been handed over multiple sectors of management by few companies as it can perform several tedious tasks in no time.
8. A.I. is also very beneficial for the law enforcement departments as it can predict faces of people by analysing only one-third of the face.
9. Artificial intelligence doesn't require any breaks hence it saves the time wasted by the human employees.
10. Many employees are replaced by the A.I. this feature increases the profit of the company.

Important points of the composition against the motion: -

1. A.I. has evolved itself in such a way that has made it a common name in every office, school or household.
2. Artificial intelligence replaces the employees of a company and hence it becomes a source for the increasing unemployment rate of the country.
3. Artificial intelligence can easily create complex programs, spreadsheets, presentations in no time. This makes the professionals of these fields deprived of their jobs.
4. Artificial intelligence can create a large number of photos and videos. This can increase the rate of cybercrimes because of deepfake videos and images.
5. Artificial intelligence makes the artists, who earn their living by making drawings or paintings, jobless.
6. Data loss may occur through the artificial intelligence.
7. Artificial intelligence can create multiple clones of itself thus it replaces the computer engineers, who invented it, from their jobs.
8. Because of its capacity of cloning or rebuilding itself, it can become more powerful than humans.

9. Humans have invented the Artificial intelligence. This fact suggests that nothing can defeat a human mind in accuracy.
10. Because of the unemployment caused by the artificial intelligence the total annual income tax received by the country reduces.

"ONLINE CLASSES ARE BETTER THAN OFFLINE CLASSES"

For the motion

The system of teaching and studying online originated mainly because of the spread of a pandemic named as covid-19. During middle of 2020 and early 2021, spread of this pandemic was at its peak because of which our nation suffered lockdowns in almost each and every part. And even after repealing of the lockdown, it was not safe for children to go to schools for carrying out studies. So, in order to prevent loss of studies of students, the schools throughout our nation decided to carry out teaching activities online with the help of internet. This approach of teaching and studying online was liked by both the teachers and the students.

This method has proved itself very beneficial for students as it allows students to study from their home. Hence, it prevents the wastage of time as well as money for travelling to their schools. Many parents go to drop their children to the schools using fuel-operated individual vehicles. While doing so, because of combustion of fuel in the internal combustion engines of the vehicles a lot of air pollutants are released which cause harm to our environment. Whereas online studies do not require such practices hence they contribute to the betterment of our environment.

Further, during the rush hours, roads are densely populated with fast moving vehicles. Because of which the chances of accidents increase. But since students do not need to travel to their schools for studies, the chances of accidents as well as the traffic density on the roads also decreases.

Online studies also benefit the students as when teachers teach students online, there is an option for recording the lectures. This option can be checked by the students for as many times they wish to. If any student misses his/her classes or is not able to understand anything related to that chapter or topic, they can easily watch the recorded lectures and understand the concerned topics. Thus, posing no serious impact on the studies of the students.

This method of teaching is also budget friendly both for students as well as schools. Because during online studies, teachers teach students without the physical classrooms. This leads to reduction in expenses of the school for providing resources such as electricity for running air-conditioners, smart boards, water coolers, computers as well as furniture such as chairs and tables. Hence, the amount of money needed for the maintenance of above-mentioned resources becomes negligible. This leads to reduction in overall fees of the school. This also makes the method budget friendly both for students as well as schools.

Also, with the help of online methods of studying, students can enrol themselves in their desired schools inside or outside the country. As they do not need to go anywhere for studying, they have opportunity to be easily taught from distant schools or colleges.

With this, I want to end my composition emphasizing about the fact that the introduction of online studies has not only helped the students and the teachers but also has helped the parents, school administration and the environment.

Against the motion

Since 2020, few terms such as online studying and online teaching have become very common. Most of the coaching institutions have already shifted to this kind of teaching method and it is also seen that the schools are also trying their best to promote online teaching and studying. After 2020 i.e. after the covid 19 pandemic, the world saw a change in the method of studies. Especially in India, all the schools shifted from physical classes to digital classes throughout the nation. This shift from the basic to new and modern form of teaching became the foundation for Ed-Tech industries to setup in India. The way of teaching students online is an interesting as well as easy to do job. Hence, when the era of pandemic ended. It left behind this modern methodology of teaching.

Online studies are not fully beneficial for the students as there are many fields in which online studies fail to fulfil their purposes such as, when students move to schools, they meet their friends and they also make new friends. This helps in enhancing the personality of students.

Further, when students go to study to schools, they leave their comfort zones. Which is very much important for making them more focused on their goals. The environment provided by the classrooms of the schools motivates students to study. Also, the vigilance of the teachers develops a kind of fear as well as affection towards the teachers because of which students perform all their tasks and activities sincerely.

While studying from home, it becomes difficult to check and administer that whether the students are really studying or not. As well as, whether they are doing their work correctly and honestly or not. However, in schools it is possible to keep an eye on the activities of the students by the teachers. Also, while studying in classrooms, it becomes easy to correct students right on the points they commit mistakes. Getting this kind of attention by the teachers through online platforms is next to impossible.

While studying online, students look into the screens of mobiles, laptops, desktop P.C.s and tablets continuously. This leads to development of strain in the eyes of the students and hence their eyes become weak. Continuous exposure to such screens may result in posing a significant damage to the vision of the students as well as the teachers.

Also, in many areas, internet connection is not very stable. Hence, the variability in the strength of internet reduces the content quality of the lectures because of which students fail to understand the topics as well as clear their doubts.

The examinations taken through the online platforms are nothing less than just a formality. As students can easily cheat and write answers to the asked questions from looking into books or surfing the internet. For these purposes physical classrooms are required.

Further, many activities such as physical sports and practical implementation of concepts (Practical examinations) of a topic cannot be performed in the online platforms or homes. For carrying out such activities, schools and teachers' guidance are required.

Also, electronic devices are not allowed inside the premises of the school. Hence schools are free from distractions so that the focus of each student is at its peak. Whereas, the online classes are basically dependent upon these electronic devices only. So, the notifications received after short intervals make it very difficult for students to focus while studying.

With this, I would like to end my composition criticizing the concept of online schooling and making this thing very clear that the temporary methods of schooling adopted during pandemic shall not be continued for the sake of the better future of India's youth.

Important points of the composition for the motion: -

1. System of teaching online originated mainly because of the spread of the covid-19 pandemic.
2. Because of the pandemic, it was not safe for the children to go to schools for carrying out their studies. So, almost all the educational institutions decided to carry out teaching process through online medium.
3. Online teaching prevents the wastage of time for travelling to schools.
4. Online teaching also prevents the wastage of money if the children use public transport or any other motor vehicle for commuting to the schools.
5. Many parents go to drop their children to the schools using fuel-operated individual vehicles. While doing so because of combustion of fuel in the internal combustion engines of the vehicles, a lot of air pollutants are released which cause harm to our environment.
6. Since students do not need to travel to their schools for studies the chances of accidents as well as the traffic density on the roads also decreases.
7. This method of teaching online is also budget friendly both for students as well as schools.
8. With the help of online methods of studying, students can enrol themselves in their desired schools inside or outside the country.

9. Online studies also benefit the students as when teachers teach students online, there is an option for recording the lectures through which the students can record the lectures for future reference.
10. Online studies have not only helped the students and the teachers but also have helped the parents, school administration and the environment.

Important points of the composition against the motion: -

1. Online studies are not fully beneficial for the students as there are many fields in which online studies fail to fulfil their purposes.
2. When students go to study to schools, they leave their comfort zones. Which is very much important for making them more focused on their goals.
3. The environment provided by the classrooms of the schools motivates students to study.
4. The vigilance of the teachers develops a kind of fear as well as affection towards the teachers because of which they perform all their tasks and activities sincerely. This vigilance is missing during online studies.
5. While studying from home, it becomes difficult to check and administer that whether the students are really studying or not.
6. During offline studies, teachers correct students right on the points when students commit mistakes. Getting this kind of attention by the teachers through online platforms is next to impossible.
7. Continuous exposure to screens may result in posing a significant damage to the vision of the students as well as teachers.
8. Electronic devices are not allowed inside the premises of the school. Hence schools are free from

distractions so that the focus of each student is at its peak.
9. The examinations taken through the online platforms are nothing less than just a formality.
10. Many activities such as physical sports and practical implementation of concepts of a topic cannot be performed in the online platforms or homes. For carrying out such activities, schools and teachers' guidance are required.

"RAINWATER HARVESTING IS THE NEED OF THE HOUR"

For all the living organisms, water is very crucial for their survival. Our Earth is called 'Blue planet' because it contains a large amount of water. But unfortunately, about 97% of the total water of the Earth is salt-water. This water cannot be used for drinking purposes. And, out of the left 3 %, only 0.7 % is available for drinking in the form of river-water, ground-water or rainwater and left 2.3 % is frozen water.

Even though India receives an appropriate amount of rainfall to carry out irrigational processes, but then also some or the other parts of India face drought like conditions throughout the year. The reason for this is overexploitation of water.

On the Earth, the primary source of water is rainwater. But we all depend on the secondary sources of water such as rivers, canals, wells etc. while being dependent on the secondary sources of water, we do not pay attention towards the conservation of primary sources. As a result, the rainwater flows through the drains to the rivers and finally it ends up meeting in seas or oceans.

In some areas, rainfall occurs for a short period of time with a heavy downpour and in some areas, it occurs for a long period of time with a very mild downpour. Further, sometimes rainfall comes very early and sometimes it gets delayed for a considerable amount of time. This causes a lot of harm to the crops on which the population of our nation sustains. In order to meet such unforeseen circumstances, rainwater harvesting becomes the need of the hour.

Rainwater harvesting helps us in storing the rainwater which could be used later when required. For carrying out rainwater harvesting there are many ways but the most common ones are recharging the underground water-table or storing the rainwater in containers after purifying it. For recharging the underground water-table, pit holes are constructed or the grasses are grown which restrict the flow of water to the drains and hence the rainwater seeps down the soil and decreases the depth of the ground water-table. In case of storing the rainwater in the containers, the water from the rooftops of the buildings seeps down through the pipelines and gets stored in the PVC or cemented tanks for future use.

During drought-like conditions, this harvested rainwater can be utilised for irrigational and other purposes. When not harvested, the rainwater gets accumulated in the low-lying areas or the drainages. This stagnant water promotes breeding of the mosquitos as well as evaporation.

The water vapours formed due to evaporation cause increase in the global warming as water vapours also contribute a lot in trapping the heat of the sun as a greenhouse gas. In cases when the water seeps down or when it is collected in a container, no evaporation takes place. Hence, the rate of evaporation decreases.

In recent years, people are stepping forward for supporting rainwater harvesting. There are many ways for harvesting the rainwater. Few best ways for harvesting rainwater are that we can store the rainwater directly in containers or we can create few holes in our ground through which rainwater can seep down and recharge the water present under the surface of the Earth.

Important points of the composition: –

1. On the Earth, the primary source of water is rainwater.
2. Our Earth is called 'Blue planet' because it contains a large amount of water.
3. About 97% of the total water of the Earth is salt-water. This water cannot be used for drinking purposes. And, out of the left 3 %, only 0.7 % is available for drinking in the form of river-water, ground-water or rainwater and left 2.3 % is frozen water.
4. Some or the other parts of India face drought like conditions throughout the year. The reason for this is over-exploitation of water.
5. If not stored properly, the rainwater flows through the drains to the rivers and finally it ends up meeting in seas or oceans.
6. In some areas, rainfall occurs for a short period of time with a heavy downpour and in some areas, it occurs for a long period of time with a very mild downpour.
7. Sometimes rainfall comes very early and sometime it gets delayed for a considerable amount of time. This causes a lot of harm to the crops on which the population of our nation sustains.
8. Rainwater harvesting helps us in storing the rainwater which could be used later when required.

9. The rainwater gets accumulated in the low-lying areas or the drainages. This stagnant water promotes breeding of the mosquitos as well as evaporation.
10. In recent years, people are stepping forward for supporting rainwater harvesting.

"RURAL AREAS AND POPULATION EXPLOSION"

With the increase in the ease of availability of the modern healthcare facilities, the population throughout the world has increased. The same has happened in our India too. But, in our nation, it is seen that the urban areas play a very short role in the increase in the rate of overall population in comparison to the rural areas. There are multiple reasons because of which the Indian rural population is growing at a very fast rate. If this increase in the rate of population will continue to rise, the availability of resources will continue to decrease and rate of inflation will rise.

In rural areas, most of the families earn their living by farming and agriculture. These families require multiple hands to help each other in the family. Hence in order to reduce the expenses made on the paid labours for getting help in the fields, these members of family help each other and the money which was to be invested for getting labours is saved. Because of this fact, most of the people in rural areas are interested in growing the number of members in their family so that these members can help them in farming and increasing the annual income of the family. But these people who support population growth, because of lack of education, do not understand that the resources are used by the members of their family throughout the year whereas labours are required for a specific amount of time. Hence, increasing population becomes more expensive for them.

Also, because all members involved in an occupation are of the same family, the labours lose their jobs and this causes increase in the rate of unemployment which further decreases the status of our nation in front of other nations.

Because of lack of education, people in the rural areas get married usually at very early ages like 21 years. This makes the reproductive time period of these people more than that of the people of the urban areas who marry at an average age of 30 years. Hence this interval between the ages of marrying plays a very significant role in the growth of population.

Since the infant mortality rate in the rural areas used to be more than that in the urban areas. Rural population still finds it safe to reproduce multiple individuals so that few of them would survive. But, with the help of modern equipment and the scientific advancement, the infant mortality rate has been decreased with a large margin even in the rural areas. And because of decreased infant mortality rate, almost all new-born infants survive. This leads to increase in the population of an area.

The rate of illiteracy is decreasing very rapidly in the rural areas but in many villages, stereotypical desires of people for male child still dominate. Hence in order to get a male child these families continue to reproduce until a male child is born without thinking of the situations that may arise because of them.

With the increase in population, it becomes difficult for individuals to make enough money to meet the requirements of their family members. Hence many people migrate to the cities in search of jobs. This leads to population explosion in the cities. This population explosion not only results in development of unhygienic conditions but also results in a significant reduction in the quantity of resources of a particular area. And if this rate of increase in population continues to rise, our farmers won't be able to produce enough quantity of the crops to feed everyone as most of the forests and farming lands have already been converted to buildings so as to accommodate so many individuals.

Although the government of India has taken many steps to make the rural population aware of the consequences of increase in population and also to decrease the illiteracy rate. But still few families continue to believe in their stereotypical ideologies.

Important points of the composition: -

1. With the increase in the ease of availability of the modern healthcare facilities, the population throughout the world has increased.
2. In our nation, it is seen that the urban areas play a very short role in the increase in the rate of overall population in comparison to the rural areas.
3. If this increase in the rate of population will continue to rise, the availability of resources will continue to decrease and rate of inflation too, will rise.
4. Most of the people in rural areas are interested in growing the number of members in their family so that these members can help them in farming or increasing the annual income of the family.
5. Because all members involved in an occupation are of the same family, the labours lose their jobs this increases the rate of unemployment.
6. This increase in rate of unemployment decreases the status of our nation in front of other nations.
7. Because of lack of education, people in the rural areas get married usually at very early ages like 21 years. This makes the reproductive time period of these people more than those who get married by the age of 30 years.
8. Since the infant mortality rate in the rural areas used to be more than that in the urban areas. Rural population still finds it safe to reproduce multiple individuals so that few of them would survive.

9. In many villages, stereotypical desires of people for the male child still dominate.
10. Many people migrate to the cities in search of jobs. This leads to population explosion in the cities.

"IMPACT OF SOCIAL MEDIA ON TEENAGERS"

Social media is nowadays being considered as a villain for children. Since the very introduction of the social media, its craze is increasing day-by-day as it is being liked by individuals of all age groups. But, especially for the teenagers, using social media is considered as nothing less than a sin. After the covid-19 pandemic, the online classes and online gaming became popular as children were prohibited to play outside their houses due to lockdown. Since the parks were closed and new television shows were also not being produced, the consumption of social media content by the children increased as it was the only means of recreation for them.

As children are very innocent, they do not understand what is good for them and what is bad for them. They easily get influenced with almost all the social media influencers and often do something which may be unsuitable for their ages or possess risk to them and their health. This effect of social media is actually dangerous for the youth. Many criminals use social media as a platform for committing cybercrimes. Since most social media platforms do not keep strict watch on the activities of its users, Cases such as cyberstalking are increasing day-by-day. We need to protect the youth from these unethical activities of the criminals.

Many social media influencers post things which contain adult contents. And protecting children from these types of contents is very important as this type of content can cause harm to the mental health of the children.

But while discussing the negative features of the social media platforms we cannot ignore the positive features. As there are always two faces of a coin, it will be our fault if we will not consider the positive features of social media.

Actually, social media is not that much wrong that children or teenagers cannot use it. It is evident from the fact that when the social media platforms got attention, there was a panic situation all over the world because of the covid-19 pandemic. The daily routine of people was ceased. Many people lost their loved ones and many had their loved ones admitted in the I.C.U. fighting from life and death. Many people lost their jobs and were sitting jobless at their homes without any income. They all suffered a great trauma. And at this very critical moment, it was the social media which helped people to overcome these traumas. It helped people to get motivated by listening to the motivational speakers. It made people laugh on watching the standup comedies videos posted by the influencers. It made it possible for the people to connect to one-another and help each other in needs such as for the arrangement of oxygen cylinders, or for reaching home, and in many other ways it continued to help people during and after the pandemic. Because of this, it prevented the splinter of the hope of living in the hearts of people from blowing-off.

The social media platforms have also helped the students in their studies during and after the covid-19 pandemic. Till today, if there occurs any doubt while studying, students can easily search for or ask their doubts and get them resolved with the help of the social media platforms. Many people often teach students using these social media platforms. With this, these platforms have also helped people in spreading education to a vast section of our society for free.

These social media platforms are also used by many e-commerce companies to advertise the products of their brands and this type of marketing also helps the companies in increasing their profits.

So, with this, I would like to end my composition suggesting the fact that we should always be careful that we look for both the positive and negative impacts of the things we are concerned about as "it is always better to have no knowledge than incomplete knowledge".

Important points of the composition: –

1. Society considers use of social media for teenagers nothing less than a sin.
2. After the covid-19 pandemic, the increased usage of mobile phones made it easy for children to reach social media.
3. Children do not easily understand what is good and bad for them.
4. The criminals take advantage of the innocence of children.
5. Children get easily attracted or influenced with the social media influencers without considering the fact that the influencers perform each and every task under the expert guidance and repeating such actions without the guidance results in causing harm to the children.
6. Criminals use social media for committing cybercrimes such as cyber stalking.
7. After the covid 19 pandemic, the social media platforms became more common. Social media helped people in arranging help from the masses. For example, many people arranged the oxygen cylinders during the pandemic with the help of the social media.
8. Students can ask questions or doubts from the people through the social media platforms.
9. Social media has also helped the e-commerce companies to advertise the products of their brands.
10. The phrase – "it is always better to have no knowledge than incomplete knowledge".

"UPI SHALL BE MADE AS THE ONLY MODE OF PAYMENT"

Few years ago, an initiative was launched by the Government of India. This initiative favoured transferring of money from one bank account to another with the help of internet. This initiative is popularly known as "UPI" in India. The full form of "UPI" is *United payments Interface.* Since this payment interface uses internet as a basic resource, it is very much liked by the youth of our nation.

This type of payment interface has many benefits. Primarily, when we pay for something in cash, we use the token currency, either the notes or the coins. But this method of making payments is quite unhygienic when observed closely. As when we touch a note, we do not know with whom it was before it came into our pocket. Had it been used by an infected person, this note would become a source or a carrier of infection to the healthy person who is the recipient. Same happens in case of coins too. So, in this reference, UPI has played an important role in preventing the spread of diseases. This made it more popular during the time of the Covid-19 pandemic.

Further, the notes or the coins we use are either printed or minted. And both these processes of minting and printing require a lot of resources, and these resources cost a lot. Hence when we use the UPI as a means of payment, the amount of money wasted in printing the notes or minting the coins is reduced and the saved money can be used for the benefit of the citizens of our nation.

In practical life, after struggling through a hard day, facing traffic jams or few bitter-words, our mental peace often gets disturbed and as a result of which, we often forget that where we have paid what amount of money. But, these types of incidents do not take place when we pay using UPI as we can easily find out our payment history or bank statements online.

If UPI is made the only mode of payments there will be many benefits to our country. As the payments made online can easily be checked by the law enforcement departments of the government, the cases concerned with corruption will stop completely. And the income tax department will easily be able to locate and find out black money. If any government official would take money from any unknown source through UPI. He/she shall have to justify the reason for the same. And also, if UPI is made as the only mode of payment, the counterfeiting of our national currency will stop completely. This will help a lot in reducing the time required to make our nation completely developed.

But, focussing on one side of any topic is not ethical, so we shall also focus on the other side i.e. on the negative effects for making UPI as the only mode of payment.

UPI is based on internet, and as we know availability of internet cannot always be permanent or at a same speed throughout. In case of thunderstorms or lightning, and in many remote or backward areas either the supply of the internet ceases or internet speed becomes variable.

Hence, if anyone has to pay in these types of situations. It becomes very difficult for the person to pay. May be this is the reason why people prefer using e-wallets more than UPI.

Also, with increase in the advancement in the field of science and technology, the advancement of criminals in the field of cybercrimes has also evolved. So, complete dependency of everyone on the internet for payments may make it easier for the cybercriminals to cause financial harm to the citizens. Hence, in order to ensure complete dependency on the internet for payments we need to make it safer first.

But, with the end of this composition, I would still say that UPI is a good initiative and it should be supported by the citizens of our nation.

Important points of the composition: –

1. The full form of UPI is "United Payments Interface".
2. UPI uses internet as a basic resource.
3. Paying in cash is somehow unhygienic. While paying in cash, a person touches a note and conveys the same to the others.
4. Co-incidentally if one person who suffering from any infection does the transaction in cash, there is a very high possibility that the recipient will also get infected with the same infection.
5. UPI became popular during the spread of the covid-19 pandemic.
6. Online mode of transaction reduces the amount of money invested in minting or printing the coins and the notes of the currency. Hence the amount of money which was to be used up for the purpose of printing or minting can be used for the benefit of the citizens of our nation.
7. If UPI is made the only mode of payment the counterfeiting of the currency will not occur at all.
8. If UPI is made the only mode of payment the law enforcement agencies can easily monitor the transactions of every citizen and hence the corruption will end and the income tax department will also be able to easily find out black money.

9. Speed of internet is always variable. And in few remote areas, the good quality network is not always available.
10. Because the UPI system is based on internet, people easily become a victim to the cybercrimes.

"C.C.T.V. CAMERAS MUST BE INSTALLED IN EVERY CLASSROOM"

Closed circuit television is a common and most widely used technology in almost every house, school and office. It consists up of a collection of devices which are termed as cameras. These cameras are collectively connected to a DVR box and a display screen. The recordings of the footages from these cameras are stored in the *Digital Video Recorder box* or briefly, 'DVR box'.

In schools, this technology serves as a helpful gadget for controlling as well as maintaining discipline in a classroom. Since classroom contains many students, in order to deal with unforeseen situations, the requirement of C.C.T.V. cameras increases.

In a classroom, there are a large number of students for the teachers to deal with. Ensuring that the class and the studies of the intelligent students are not hampered, teachers regulate the class and maintain discipline. But still, the mischievous students of the classroom find out ways to disturb the class whenever they find that teacher is busy in teaching. These students cause some or the other nuisance and then disappear in the scope of the population density of the class. And because of these mischievous students, the ones who are innocent, are given punishments. Thus, to ensure that the innocent ones are not punished as well as the discipline of the class is maintained, the footages of C.C.T.V. recordings can be used as evidence.

Further, in order to know the behaviour of teachers towards their pupils, their way of interaction with the students and the status of the completion of the syllabus, this technology has no other supplementary solution.

During early morning, when the teachers are not in the classroom. Few mischievous students cause harm to the property of school by either writing inappropriate words on the desks and chairs or by breaking the glasses of the windows. With the help of the C.C.T.V. cameras, it becomes easy to find the sources or the doers of these nuisances and then subject these sources to the penalties for the loss caused by them.

For teachers also, it becomes a very unpractical approach to say that they have to control a class of hundred students together ensuring that no hindrance is caused in the class because of any student and also teach at the same time. Being human beings, teachers too cannot perform multiple tasks together, they can either teach or can monitor the activities of the students in the class and maintain the discipline. But, in case, any nuisance occurs in a classroom, teachers are considered as the sole responsible body for the nuisance. Hence, to ensure that the teachers are easily able to carry out their job, C.C.T.V. cameras act as a surveillance which helps in finding out the responsible bodies behind any nuisance.

Thus, in addition to the points mentioned previously, I would like to add another benefit of these cameras.

Whenever any mischievous thought arises in mind of anyone, the presence of C.C.T.V. camera indicates that the source of any nuisance will be easily identified with the help of the camera. This thought forbids people from getting indulged in such activities. By this, it ensures discipline in class.

Important points of the composition: -

1. Closed circuit television cameras are also called as C.C.T.V. cameras.
2. C.C.T.V. camera is a common and widely used technology in almost every house, school and office.
3. C.C.T.V. cameras are collectively connected to a DVR box and a display screen.
4. This technology helps in controlling as well as maintaining discipline in a classroom so, in order to deal with unforeseen situations, the requirement of C.C.T.V. cameras increases.
5. Ensuring that the class and the studies of the intelligent students are not hampered, teachers regulate the class and maintain discipline. But still, the mischievous students of the classroom find out ways to disturb the class. This can be prevented with the help of C.C.T.V. Cameras.
6. It becomes easier to find out from where the teacher had left the chapter with the help of the previous recordings of the C.C.T.V. cameras.
7. It becomes a very unpractical approach to say that teachers have to control a class of hundred students together ensuring that no hindrance is caused in the class.
8. The presence of C.C.T.V. cameras indicates that the source of any nuisance will be easily identified.

9. C.C.T.V. cameras protect the innocents from being punished for offence which is not done by them.
10. C.C.T.V. cameras helps the teachers in performing the job they are responsible for.

"PARENTS SHOULD NOT BE STRICT TO THEIR CHILDREN"

Childhood is considered as the golden era of life of an individual. It is so, because during this stage children celebrate each and every second of their life. They get excited while watching butterflies and they get sad when they see anyone crying. They enjoy and learn lessons in each and every second of their life. But if at this stage they are not treated with care and affection by their parents, they start considering their parents as outsiders. Because of which, children fail to disclose their feelings and emotions in front of their parents.

Parents are considered as God for their off-springs. It is so as they are the only true well-wishers of their children in the world, which is full of selfishness. They guide their children in each and every situation with the help of their experiences. Parents love and care for their off-springs but, they often fail to show their affection. They try to be rude or strict to their children for the sake of their bright future only. But, the immature mindset of children fails to understand the intentions of the parents towards them.

This kind of attitude of parents towards their children reduces self-confidence of children and this makes them prone to more risks. As at this age, children start gaining experiences about the world and their surroundings. These experiences help them to take decisions to prevent themselves from any kind of loss throughout their lives. Because of the fear developed in minds of these children, they avoid discussing about their problems or the mistakes made by them. Because of which, these children fail to get correct guidance from their parents and they suffer huge losses.

At the initial ages, when children are scolded because of doing any activity which is harmful for them, a kind of interest is developed in the minds of these children to try and see the outcomes of such activities. In deficiency of proper family bond and guidance, these children start doing such harmful activities in absence of their parents. And when these activities show their results, it becomes too late to act upon them.

Parents when treat their off-springs friendly, they understand the reason because of which they were forbidden from doing any particular activity. And in such conditions, children feel free to disclose any issue in front of their parents as there is no fear of getting scolded for their questions. Whenever a problem is being faced or a mistake has been committed by children, they seek advice of their parents and get out of the problems easily.

So, it is very important for the parents to not to be strict with their off-springs. And, for the children also to not to consider their parents as their enemies. I would like to end this passage with a line which is as follows: -

"It may happen that the decisions of parents are not always perfect. But it will never happen that their intentions are incorrect".

Important points of the composition: –

1. Childhood is considered as the golden era of life of an individual.
2. Parents are considered as God for their off-springs.
3. Parents try to be rude or strict to their children for the sake of their bright future only.
4. The immature mindset of children fails to understand the intentions of the parents towards them.
5. Rude attitude of parents towards their children reduces self-confidence of children and this makes them prone to more risks.
6. At the initial ages, when children are scolded because of doing any activity which is harmful for them a kind of interest is developed in the minds of these children to try and see the outcomes of such activities.
7. Because of the fear developed from the rude attitude in minds of these children, they avoid discussing about their problems or the mistakes made by them.
8. In absence of proper familiar bond, children fail get correct guidance from their parents and they suffer huge losses.
9. It is very important for the parents to not to be strict with their off-springs. And, for the children also to not to consider their parents as their enemies.
10. "It may happen that decisions of parents are not always perfect. But it will never happen that their intentions are incorrect".

"ROLE AND BENEFITS OF TELEVISION IN THE SOCIETY"

It seems almost impossible to imagine a life without television in this modern era. But there are many places which still lack availability of television. In the vicinity of modern and new technology, we forget significance of the things which we use on a daily basis. Most of us start our day with the television and end with it too. We often forget that the things which are basic necessity for us may be luxury for others. In the beginning, televisions were a part of luxury for each and everyone. But with the advancement of our country in the field of technology, televisions became common in almost every household.

The invention of television proved to be a boon for people as it was the best way for recreation. Television not only acted as a source for recreation but also as a source for spreading news to masses. With the help of television, it became easy to provide the people with the details of the activities taking place throughout the nation. For example, if there is a misunderstanding between two groups, it is easier to end the deadlock between the two with the help of the news. It also acts as a communicator between the government and the citizens of India. News through television can be easily communicated to the people without much delay as compared to the newspaper. It makes it easier to communicate any important instruction or to make the general people aware about the new policies of the government with the help of the news through television.

With the increase in the popularity of television, the daily serials also became popular. This made it possible to reduce the unemployment rate of our nation by employing a number of professionals for producing successive episodes of a serial. These professionals include cameramen, actors, makeup persons and many other individuals from different fields and expertise. While interacting with television, when people watch any show or advertisement given by a company, the channels which are platform to these serials and advertisements generate revenue which also results in providing a significant amount of tax to our nation. Hence, television shows also help in the development of our nation.

Television serials often convey good moral values which are carried to the youth. Following which, can result in making every individual a gentle and a humble personality. It helps the younger ones in learning the lessons of life and know that the world around them is not exactly same as they think it to be. This shows a positive impact of television on the Indian societies.

In the very beginning, Doordarshan was the only channel which was owned by the Government of India. Now there are many branches of Doordarshan. They broadcast few serials which help the farmers of our nation by making them aware of the new and modern farming techniques and the crops. Not only for the farmers but also for the students of our nation, many serials for their education are also being broadcasted.

Many serials also make us aware of the history and the heritage of our nation.

Television broadcasts movies and comedy shows. Broadcasting movies makes it possible for the people to save money which was to be invested in buying tickets of the theatre for watching the same movie. And comedy shows help people a lot by reducing their mental stress when they laugh.

Ending with the composition, I want to include last point which says that, nowadays, television is not much respected in front of other resources by the youth. In place of watching the serials based on moral values, people love to watch reels and other videos which do not donate much to our knowledge and also contain sexual or adult content which can be harmful for the children.

Important points of the composition: -

1. It seems almost impossible to imagine a life without television in this modern era.
2. In the vicinity of modern and new technology we forget significance of the things which we use on a daily basis.
3. The invention of television proved to be a boon for people as it was the best way for recreation.
4. With the help of television, it became easy to provide the people with the details of the activities taking place throughout the nation.
5. Television acts as a communicator between the government and the citizens of India.
6. Television makes it easier to make the general people aware about the new policies of government with the help of the news through it.
7. With the increase in the popularity of the television, the daily serials also became popular. This made it possible to reduce the unemployment rate of our nation by employing a number of professionals for producing successive episodes of a serial.
8. The advertisements shown by the channels through the television contribute in the well-being of our nation by providing the tax on the revenue generated by them.
9. The television serials often convey good moral values which are carried to the youth. Following

which, can result in making every individual a gentle and a humble personality.
10. In the very beginning, Doordarshan was the only channel which was owned by the Government of India. It broadcasts few serials which help the farmers of our nation to be aware of the new and modern farming techniques and the crops.

"INCREASING GLOBAL WARMING IS A WARNING"

Global warming is a phenomenon which regulates the temperature of the surface of the Earth. In the absence of this phenomenon, life on the surface of the Earth would be impossible as the Earth would have become a cold vast desert. Global warming can also be considered as a necessary evil. It is necessary as it regulates and increases the temperature of the surface of the Earth. Thus, making it an inhabitable planet. And evil, as it can lead to a large amount of destruction because of increase in the overall temperature of the surface of the Earth.

The significant increase monitored in the rate of increase of global warming is result of anti-natural activities of human beings. These anti-natural activities such as deforestation, mining, overgrazing, slash and burn farming and so on cause a considerable amount of damage to the materials of the nature.

The increase in the global temperature is alarming. It is of urgent importance to look into this matter and take necessary steps. The main source of global warming is greenhouse effect. And this greenhouse effect is caused by few substances present in our atmosphere, which are carbon dioxide, water vapours, oxides of nitrogen and sulphur and other particulates. Production of these substances shall be reduced so as to defend ourselves from the scourge of natural disasters.

If no action will be taken to prevent global warming, the surface temperature will continue to rise. This rise in temperature will result in melting of glaciers, increased rate of evaporation, damaged and low-quality of crops and so on. Hence, damaged or bad-quality yields of crops will also result in famines throughout the globe. This also effects the animals as their natural cycles are set with respect to the climatic conditions but change in climatic conditions disturbs the proper functioning of their body organs.

Melting of glaciers will increase the sea-water level which will result in decrease in the amount of drinkable water present on the Earth's surface and submergence of parts of peninsular regions under the surface of the sea-water.

Further, the increase in the global temperatures will increase the rate of evaporation. This will lead to formation of water vapours and as water vapours are one of the sources of global warming, the rise in global warming will continue.

Hence, it is very important for us to understand the alarm of nature and instead of sitting and waiting for mass destruction, we should step forward to aware people to take required steps and prevent global warming by asking them to use cycles, buses or metros instead of individual vehicles. To promote afforestation and reforestation and also to adopt new and better farming methods so as to prevent wastage of water. The Government of our nation has also taken important steps to prevent the increase in the rate of global warming by promoting the use of vehicles which run on batteries, construction of metros in required areas, carrying out afforestation and ensuring us that we can altogether make a change in the current conditions of our surroundings for the benefit of us as well as our future generations.

Important points of the composition: -

1. Global warming regulates optimum temperature of the surface of the Earth.
2. Global warming is a necessary evil.
    - Necessary, as it regulates the minimum temperature
    - Evil, as it leads to a large amount of destruction
3. Increase in overall temperature leads to a large amount of destruction.
4. The increase monitored in global warming is a result of Anti-Natural activities of human beings. Here, the word 'anti-natural activities' refers to the activities which are not in favour of nature.
5. Slash and burn farming is a kind of farming in which the crop residues left after harvesting are burnt in air.
6. The increase in global warming is alarming.
7. Main source of global warming is greenhouse effect.
8. And, the main sources of greenhouse effect are carbon dioxide, water vapours, oxides of nitrogen and sulphur and the particulates present in air.
9. In absence of any action against increasing global warming, the rise in temperature will result in melting of glaciers.
10. Afforestation and reforestation are the most helpful and significant methods for reducing global warming.

"PRIVATIZATION AND ITS IMPACT"

Privatization is always considered as an effective method for putting a full-stop on corruption. Privatization actually means the process of handing over the government-owned sectors to the private organisations. By this process, the burden of managing various governmentally-owned sectors gets reduced for the government.

But it is often seen that after the privatizing any sector, the primary aim of the sector changes from helping the people of the country to earning profits from the people of the country. From the aim of increasing the profits it can be easily understood that these private organisations may increase the charges for the services they provide. And the government will also not be able to interfere in these matters as there is no control of government on these organisations. This will result in causing harm to the people in place of helping them.

Private organisations focus on reducing the number of employees so that their expenses like paying salaries and allowances to the employees get reduced. This act of these organisations increases the work-pressure on the employees as well as the act of removing the employees from the job leads to increase in the rate of unemployment of our country.

The private organisations mainly focus on developing and providing resources to the areas which contribute a lot in their overall revenues.

Hence, this provides a way to the employees of these organisations to provide services to the consumers of the less contributing areas without the official permission from the organisations in exchange of some bribe. This leads to increase in the corruption in these private organisations too.

Many sectors of our nation need to be owned by the government in order to protect the rights of the citizens. For example, if all the governmental schools will be privatized, the students who can afford the high cost of the private schools will shift from the governmental schools to the private schools. But those who cannot afford the high fees charged by the private institutions will be deprived of their educational rights. Hence, for the sake of the future of the youth of India, few sectors must always remain under the control of the government.

As the private organisations always work for their profit, they do not provide as much benefits as provided by the governmental organisations to the citizens.

Because of privatization, it becomes difficult for the government to regulate that whether all the private organisations are providing reservation to the citizens who are eligible for it or not. If this happens, the people who are differently-abled will be removed from their jobs as the private organisations focus on increasing their profits in place of focussing on the welfare of the citizens of our nation as the governmental organisations do.

Hence, with this, I would like to end my composition indicating towards the fact that privatization is a way, with the help of which the pressure on the government is reduced so that the government can focus on the topics of national importance. But, it is difficult to say that privatization can guarantee the development of the people of the nation or not.

Important points of the composition: –

1. Privatization actually means the process of handing over the government sectors to the private organisations.
2. By privatization, the burden of managing various governmentally-owned sectors gets reduced for the government.
3. But it is often seen that after the privatizing any sector, the primary aim of the sector changes from helping the people of the country to earning profits from the people of the country.
4. From the aim of increasing the profits it can be easily understood that after privatizing, these private organisations may increase the charges for the services they provide.
5. Private organisations focus on reducing the number of employees so that their expenses like paying salary and allowances to the employees get reduced.
6. When the private organisations decrease the number of employees, the work-pressure on the employees as well as the rate of unemployment of the country increases.
7. The private organisations mainly focus on developing and providing resources to the areas which contribute a lot in their overall revenues.

8. Many sectors of our nation need to be owned by the government in order to protect the rights of their citizens.

9. As the private organisations always work for their profit, they do not provide as much benefits as provided by the governmental organisations to the citizens.

10. Privatization is a way, with the help of which the pressure on the government is reduced so that the government can focus on the topics of national importance.

www.ingramcontent.com/pod-product-compliance
Lightning Source LLC
LaVergne TN
LVHW061553070526
838199LV00077B/7032